To

From

A DON'T SWEAT THE SMALL STUFF Treasury

Also by the Author

Don't Sweat the Small Stuff at Work
Don't Sweat the Small Stuff with Your Family
Don't Worry, Make Money
Don't Sweat the Small Stuff . . . And It's All Small Stuff
Slowing Down to the Speed of Life
(with Joseph Bailey)
Handbook for the Heart (with Benjamin Shield)
Handbook for the Soul (with Benjamin Shield)
Shortcut Through Therapy
You Can Feel Good Again
You Can Be Happy No Matter What

Don't Sweat the Small Stuff Treasuries:
A Special Selection for Graduates
A Special Selection for Teachers
A Special Selection for Fathers

A
DON'T SWEAT THE SMALL STUFF
Treasury

A Special Selection for Mothers

Richard Carlson, Ph.D.

Andrews McMeel Publishing

Kansas City

 For information, write Andrews McMeel Publishing, an Andrews McMeel Universal company, 4520 Main Street, Kansas City, Missouri 64111.

www.andrewsmcmeel.com

ISBN: 0-740-70162-2

Library of Congress Catalog Card Number: 99-60282

Contents

Introduction

I'm an "old-fashioned guy." To me, moms are it, angels in disguise! There is no one more important to me than my own mom, Barbara, and Kris, the mother of my two children. It seems obvious that there is no job more important or significant than being a mom and no greater contribution that a person could make than being a loving mother.

I have enormous respect for mothers and sincere gratitude for the sacrifice, loyalty, and love that almost all mothers offer their children. Without moms, none of us would be here—and without patient and dedicated moms, our world would be in complete chaos. Indeed, mothers keep our world intact. They are responsible for so much of the good in our world, and they deserve to be honored and admired.

I often chuckle when someone tells me, "You must get really tired with your busy schedule." As a man, I see the humor in this typical comment because everything is relative. A work day might last eight hours or so, complete with a lunch break—but a mother's job takes place 24 hours a day, 365 days a year! And what's more, a mother is still a mother, even after her children grow up and move away.

Understandably, with all the responsibilities of being a mother comes a great deal of stress that only she can understand. And because there are so many big and important issues that a mother must deal with, sometimes on a daily basis, it's critical that she learn to keep the smaller things from overwhelming her. I've been told by thousands of moms that learning to stop sweating the small stuff has been enormously helpful in their efforts to be the best mom possible, to keep their stress under control, and to help them enjoy the gift of being a parent.

It's for this reason that I have created this little book especially for moms. With feedback from lots of mothers, I have carefully selected strategies from each of my *Don't Sweat the Small Stuff* books that seem to be most useful in helping moms become less stressed, happier people.

If you are a mom, I send you my best wishes and a great big hug! Thank you for being the best mom you know how to be. If this book helps you, even slightly, in becoming more relaxed and happy, it was worth putting together. Again, thank you for being a mom and for being you.

Treasure yourself,

Richard Carlson

1.

Make Peace with Imperfection

I've yet to meet an absolute perfectionist whose life was filled with inner peace. The need for perfection and the desire for inner tranquility conflict with each other. Whenever we are attached to having something a certain way, better than it already is, we are, almost by definition, engaged in a losing battle. Rather than being content and grateful for what we have, we are focused on what's wrong with something and our need to fix it. When we are zeroed in on what's wrong, it implies that we are dissatisfied, discontent.

Whether it's related to ourselves—a disorganized closet, a scratch on the car, an imperfect accomplishment, a few pounds we would like to lose—or someone else's "imperfections"—the way someone looks, behaves, or lives their life—the very act of focusing on imperfection pulls us away from our goal of being kind and gentle. This strategy has nothing to do with ceasing to do your very best but with being overly attached and focused on what's wrong with life. It's about realizing that while there's always a better way to do something, this doesn't mean that you can't enjoy and appreciate the way things already are.

The solution here is to catch yourself when you fall into your habit of insisting that things should be other than they are. Gently remind yourself that life is okay the way it is, right now. In the absence of your judgment, everything would be fine. As you begin to eliminate your need for perfection in all areas of your life, you'll begin to discover the perfection in life itself.

2.

Ask Yourself the Question, "Will This Matter a Year from Now?"

Almost every day I play a game with myself that I call "time warp." I made it up in response to my consistent, erroneous belief that what I was all worked up about was really important.

To play "time warp," all you have to do is imagine that whatever circumstance you are dealing with isn't happening right now but a year from now. Then simply ask yourself, "Is this situation really as important as I'm making it out to be?" Once in a great while it may be—but a vast majority of the time, it simply isn't.

Whether it be an argument with your spouse, child, or boss, a mistake, a lost opportunity, a lost wallet, a work-related rejection, or a sprained ankle, chances are, a year from now you aren't going to care. It will be one more irrelevant detail in your life. While this simple game won't solve all your problems, it can give you an enormous amount of needed perspective. I find myself laughing at things that I used to take far too seriously. Now, rather than using up my energy feeling angry and overwhelmed, I can use it instead on spending time with my wife and children or engaging in creative thinking.

3.

Lower Your Tolerance to Stress

It seems that we have it backward in our society. We tend to look up to people who are under a great deal of stress, who can handle loads of stress, and those who are under a great deal of pressure. When someone says, "I've been working really hard," or "I'm really stressed out," we are taught to admire, even emulate their behavior. In my work as a stress consultant I hear the proud words "I have a very high tolerance to stress" almost every day. It probably won't come as a surprise that when these stressed-out people first arrive at my office, more often than not, what they are hoping for are strategies to *raise* their tolerance to stress even higher so they can handle even more!

Fortunately, there is an inviolable law in our emotional environment that goes something like this: Our current level of stress will be exactly that of our tolerance to stress. You'll notice that the people who say, "I can handle lots of stress" will always be under a great deal of it! So, if you teach people to raise their tolerance to stress, that's exactly what will happen. They will accept even more confusion and responsibility until again, their external level of stress matches that of their tolerance. Usually it takes a crisis of some kind to wake up a stressed-out person to their own craziness—a spouse leaves, a health issue emerges, a serious addiction takes over their life—something happens that jolts them into a search for a new kind of strategy.

It may seem strange, but if you were to enroll in the average stress management workshop, what you would probably learn is to *raise* your tolerance to stress. It seems that even stress consultants are stressed out!

What you want to start doing is noticing your stress early, *before* it gets out of hand. When you feel your mind moving too quickly, it's time to back off and regain your bearings. When your schedule is getting out of hand, it's a signal that it's time to slow down and reevaluate what's important rather than power through everything on the list. When you're feeling out of control and resentful of all you have to do, rather than roll up your sleeves and "get to it," a better strategy is to relax, take a few deep breaths, and go for a short walk. You'll find that when you catch yourself getting too stressed out—early, before it gets out of control—your stress will be like the proverbial snowball rolling down the hill. When it's small, it's manageable and easy to control. Once it gathers momentum, however, it's difficult, if not impossible, to stop.

There's no need to worry that you won't get it all done. When your mind is clear and peaceful and your stress level is reduced, you'll be more effective and you'll have more fun. As you lower your tolerance to stress, you will find that you'll have far less stress to handle, as well as creative ideas for handling the stress that is left over.

4.

Choose Your Battles Wisely

"Choose your battles wisely" is a popular phrase in parenting but is equally important in living a contented life. It suggests that life is filled with opportunities to choose between making a big deal out of something or simply letting it go, realizing it doesn't really matter. If you choose your battles wisely, you'll be far more effective in winning those that are truly important.

Certainly there will be times when you will want or need to argue, confront, or even fight for something you believe in. Many people, however, argue, confront, and fight over practically anything, turning their lives into a series of battles over relatively "small stuff." There is so much frustration in living this type of life that you lose track of what is truly relevant.

The tiniest disagreement or glitch in your plans can be made into a big deal if your goal (conscious or unconscious) is to have everything work out in your favor. In my book, this is nothing more than a prescription for unhappiness and frustration.

The truth is, life is rarely exactly the way we want it to be, and other people often don't act as we would like them to. Moment to moment, there are aspects of life that we like and others that we don't. There are always going to be people who disagree with you, people who do things differently, and things that don't work out. If you fight against this principle of life, you'll spend most of your life fighting battles.

A more peaceful way to live is to decide consciously which battles are worth fighting and which are better left alone. If your primary goal isn't to have everything work out perfectly but instead to live a relatively stress-free life, you'll find that most battles pull you *away from* your most tranquil feelings. Is it really important that you prove to your spouse that you are right and she is wrong, or that you confront someone simply because it appears as though he or she has made a minor mistake? Does your preference of which restaurant or movie to go to matter enough to argue over it? Does a small scratch on your car really warrant a suit in small claims court? Does the fact that your neighbor won't park his car on a different part of the street have to be discussed at your family dinner table? These and thousands of other small things are what many people spend their lives fighting about. Take a look at your own list. If it's like mine used to be, you might want to reevaluate your priorities.

If you don't want to "sweat the small stuff," it's critical that you choose your battles wisely. If you do, there will come a day when you'll rarely feel the need to do battle at all.

5.

See the Glass as Already Broken (and Everything Else Too)

This is a Buddhist teaching that I learned over twenty years ago. It has provided me, again and again, with greatly needed perspective to guide me toward my goal of a more accepting self.

The essence of this teaching is that all of life is in a constant state of change. Everything has a beginning and everything has an end. Every tree begins with a seed and will eventually transform back into earth. Every rock is formed and every rock will vanish. In our modern world, this means that every car, every machine, every piece of clothing is created and that all will wear out and crumble; it's only a matter of when. Our bodies are born and they will die. A glass is created and will eventually break.

There is peace to be found in this teaching. When you expect something to break, you're not surprised or disappointed when it does. Instead of becoming immobilized when something is destroyed, you feel grateful for the time you have had.

The easiest place to start is with the simple things, a glass of water, for example. Pull out your favorite drinking glass. Take a moment to look at and appreciate its beauty and all it does for you. Now, imagine that same glass as already broken, shattered all over the floor. Try to maintain the perspective that, in time, everything disintegrates and returns to its initial form.

Obviously, no one wants their favorite drinking glass, or anything else, to be broken. This philosophy is not a prescription for becoming passive or apathetic, but for making peace with the way things are. When your drinking glass does break, this philosophy allows you to maintain your perspective. Rather than thinking, "Oh my God," you'll find yourself thinking, "Ah, there it goes." Play with this awareness and you'll find yourself not only keeping your cool but appreciating life as never before.

6.

Cut Yourself Some Slack

Each of the strategies in this book is geared toward helping you become more relaxed, peaceful, and loving. One of the most important pieces of this puzzle, however, is to remember that your goal is to stay relaxed, to not get too worked up or concerned about how you are doing. Practice the strategies, keep them in mind, yet don't worry about being perfect. Cut yourself some slack! There will be many times when you lose it, when you revert to being uptight, frustrated, stressed, and reactive—get used to it. When you do, it's okay. Life is a process—just one thing after another. When you lose it, just start again.

One of the most common mistakes I see when

people are attempting to become more inwardly peaceful is that they become frustrated by little setbacks. An alternative is to see your mistakes as learning opportunities, ways to navigate your growth and perspective. Say to yourself, "Woops, I lost it again. Oh well, next time I'll handle it differently." Over time, you'll notice drastic changes in your responses to life, but it won't happen all at once.

I once heard of a proposed book title that sums up the message of this strategy: *I'm Not Okay, You're Not Okay, and That's Okay.* Give yourself a break. No one is going to bat 100 percent, or even close to it. All that's important is that, generally speaking, you are doing your best and that you are moving in the right direction. When you can learn to keep your perspective and to stay loving toward yourself, even when you prove you are human, you'll be well on your way to a happier life.

7.

Fill Your Life with Love

I don't know anyone who doesn't want a life filled with love. In order for this to happen, the effort must start within us. Rather than waiting for other people to provide the love we desire, *we* must be a vision and a source of love. We must tap into our own loving-kindness in order to set an example for others to follow suit.

It has been said that "the shortest distance between two points is an intention." This is certainly true with regard to a life filled with love. The starting point or foundation of a life filled with love is the desire and commitment to be a source of love. Our attitude, choices, acts of kindness, and willingness to be the first to reach out will take us toward this goal.

The next time you find yourself frustrated at the lack of love in your own life or at the lack of love in the world, try an experiment. Forget about the world and other people for a few minutes. Instead, look into your own heart. Can you become a source of greater love? Can you think loving thoughts for yourself and others? Can you extend these loving thoughts outward toward the rest of the world—even to people whom you feel don't deserve it?

By opening your heart to the possibility of greater love, and by making yourself a source of love (rather than getting love) as a top priority, you will be taking an important step in getting the love you desire. You'll also discover something truly remarkable. The more love you give, the more you will receive. As you put more emphasis on being a loving person, which is something you can control—and less emphasis on receiving love, which is something you can't control—you'll find that you have plenty of love in your life. Soon you'll discover one of the greatest secrets in the world: Love is its own reward.

8.

Do One Thing at a Time

The other day I was driving on the freeway and noticed a man who, while driving in the fast lane, was shaving, drinking a cup of coffee, and reading the newspaper! "Perfect," I thought to myself, as just that morning I was trying to think of an appropriate example to point out the craziness of our frenzied society.

How often do we try to do more than one thing at once? We have cordless phones that are supposed to make our lives easier, but in some respects, they make our lives more confusing. My wife and I were at a friend's home for dinner a while ago and noticed her talking on the phone while simultaneously answering the door, checking on dinner, and changing her daughter's diaper (after she washed her hands, of course)! Many of us have the same tendency when we're speaking to someone and our mind is somewhere else, or when we're doing three or four chores all at the same time.

When you do too many things at once, it's impossible to be present-moment oriented. Thus, you not only lose out on much of the potential enjoyment of what you are doing, but you also become far less focused and effective.

An interesting exercise is to block out periods of time where you commit to doing only one thing at a time. Whether you're washing dishes, talking on the phone, driving a car, playing with your child, talking to your spouse, or reading a magazine, try to focus only on that one thing. Be present in what you are doing. Concentrate. You'll notice two things beginning to happen. First, you'll actually enjoy what you are doing, even something mundane like washing dishes or cleaning out a closet. When you're focused, rather than distracted, it enables you to become absorbed and interested in your activity, whatever it might be. Second, you'll be amazed at how quickly and efficiently you'll get things done. Since I've become more present-moment oriented, my skills have increased in virtually all areas of my life—writing, reading, cleaning house, and speaking on the phone. You can do the same thing. It all starts with your decision to do one thing at a time.

9.

Remind Yourself Frequently What Your Children Really Want

Let's face it. Your kids don't really care if you're a flight attendant, a salesperson, a waitress, a computer expert, or a chef. I can tell you from firsthand experience that they are not impressed if you are an author or a busy professional. My guess is that my kids would be equally *un*-impressed with me if I were a doctor, lawyer, or even a movie star. The fact that you work hard and sacrifice in their behalf may be appreciated, but not nearly to the extent that any of us feel is appropriate and deserved. No, what really matters to kids is your time—and your willingness to listen and love unconditionally. Period!

It's one thing to say "My kids are the most important part of my life," and it's something else altogether to back that statement up with actions. I know this isn't easy, and I also know that there are many great and often legitimate excuses why we can't make our kids our top priority, but the fact remains: Our kids don't want our external successes, they want and need our love.

This is not a strategy designed to make you feel guilty about how little time you have for your kids. Believe me, I often feel guilty myself when I have to leave for the airport before my own children have even gotten out of bed, or when I have to take an important phone call at dinnertime or miss a school play due to other plans. The goal of this strategy is not about guilt, it's about love. It's a friendly reminder that, although parenting can seem overwhelming at times and you might think it will last forever—it won't. Instead, you have a short window of opportunity in which to spend time together and develop a mutually loving and respectful relationship before your children are grown up and out on their own.

At times it's been helpful to me, and I believe it might be helpful to you, to be reminded that what our kids *really* want isn't our money or our success—or our constant reminders of how hard we work. What they really want is us. Obviously, this doesn't mean you don't need to earn a living or that success isn't (or shouldn't be) important, only that, to our kids, these things are secondary. I doubt very much that any of us, on our deathbeds, will wish we had spent even more time at the office or in pursuit of our dreams, but I suspect that many of us will regret not spending more quality time with our children. Knowing this is the case, why not make a change, however slight, in our priorities?

What our children really want (and need) is our love. They want us to listen to their stories without something else on our minds and without rushing to be somewhere else, to watch their soccer games not because we feel obligated to do so but because there is genuinely no place we'd rather be. They want us to hold them, read to them, be with them. They want to be the center of our universe.

Just this morning, I was with a good friend of mine discussing how quickly our children are growing up. It reminded me of how precious my own children, and all children, are. In that moment, I made a commitment to myself to keep my priorities straight, however inconvenient it may be. I hope you'll make a similar commitment.

10.

Have a Favorite Family Charity

Very few activities can bring a family closer together than the act of giving. We have found that having a favorite family charity is a fun way to do just this. Whether there are just two of you or ten, the idea is to get everyone in your family involved in the selection and ongoing giving process. (Obviously, if you live alone, you can do the same thing by yourself or with a friend.)

Our favorite family charity is Children, Inc., out of Richmond, Virginia; (800) 538-5381. It's an organization ideally suited for this purpose because it's easy to get everyone involved. Your family gets to meet, through the mail, a special child whom you all get to help and, and this is important, get to know.

Both you and your kids can send letters, photos, and pictures back and forth to the child you are helping and meet a new friend in the process.

Almost any charity can be an ideal opportunity to bring a family closer together. Rather than simply writing a check and putting it in the mail, bring your family into the process. Get a corporate brochure and show your children who it is you're trying to help and why. Discuss the work that the organization is doing and applaud it together. If you are sending money, let the kids see you write the check. Maybe they can put the check in the envelope, or the envelope in the mailbox. Share with them where the money is going and what it is going to do. Ask your children who they would most like to help and why. Is it children, the elderly, the homeless, or the hungry? Or would they like to make a contribution to the search for the cure for cancer or blindness?

Would they like to help stray animals or community development? This strategy gives your family the opportunity to discuss the needs in your community and in our world. It's a demonstration of your love. It's fun and rewarding, as well as helpful.

If you can't afford to give money, your family can still come together around giving. Perhaps your church or local shelter needs some help. A church in our neighborhood makes bag lunches for homeless people every Saturday. What a great way to spend a morning with your family.

What you do isn't as important as doing something. Giving of any kind feels good and brings people together, especially families. I hope you'll give this strategy a try. It will bring your family closer together and reinforce your most important values, and if each family does its own little part, we can make the world a better place.

11.

Recognize When Someone Doesn't Have an Eye for Something

You may have heard the expression, "He doesn't have the eye for it." In case you haven't, it means that the person you are referring to literally can't see what you are talking about; he or she can't understand or internalize it. For example, I remember trying to teach my oldest daughter to add two numbers together. Like the rest of us, before she saw how the principle of addition works in real life, she was stuck using her fingers and anything else necessary to add the numbers together. But, like magic, the moment it clicked, the instant she developed the eye for it, she was on her way.

Needless to say, it would have been foolish (and

cruel) to get angry at her for not having the eye for math before she was developmentally ready. Instead, like most caring parents, my wife and I tried to be patient and allow her the necessary time to digest and understand the material.

It's easy to see how relevant having the eye for something is when we're talking about a five- or six-year-old's learning to add. It's something else entirely when we assume that someone should know something, yet it's every bit as important. For example, if you have a sloppy spouse, you probably assume (perhaps incorrectly) that he (or she) truly understands what it means to clean something up—or to live within a budget. You might make similar categorical assumptions about your children over such things as the meaning of quiet, patience, being nice, and other things you and I take for granted. The truth is, however, that many of the things we assume are general knowledge are nothing of the sort. In many instances, the problem *isn't* that a person doesn't want to, or is unwilling to, help but simply that he or she doesn't have the eye for what you are asking him or her to do. It's like you're speaking different languages.

When you take this possibility into consideration, your level of frustration will drop dramatically. Perspective and compassion will replace your demands and judgments. Rather than acting out from a place of stress, you'll be more likely to become a patient teacher, a participant in the process of helping another person develop the eye for something. The person you are dealing with will become much easier to work with. You'll be bringing out the best in him or her, rather than the worst.

My wife had an interesting realization about one of our favorite baby-sitters. Although she was an excellent sitter with the kids, we would come home from a night out and the kitchen would look like a bomb had just struck! We were constantly reminding her to clean up any messes she made, to which she would respond, "No problem." Yet, we'd come home to the same giant mess each and every time. We were getting very frustrated and were considering not using her again when Kris had the insight that the sitter might honestly *not know* what we mean by "clean it all up." To our great surprise, Kris was right. To our baby-sitter, the kitchen was as clean as it needed to be. Apparently, her own kitchen frequently looked messy. It wasn't treated as a big deal in her home. But to us, it was a big deal.

This story has a happy ending. Kris and I spent about thirty minutes showing her exactly what we expected and how to go about it. To this day, the kitchen has been spotless every time we've come home from a date. The secret wasn't to yell and scream or to get frustrated and fire her—it was to help her develop the eye for a clean kitchen. Experiment with this one and you'll solve many of your day-to-day issues, quickly and easily.

12.

Create a New Relationship with Someone You Already Know

It's quite common for us to get into habits with our family members and anyone else we happen to live with. These habits include, but are by no means limited to: overreacting, defensive communication, blaming, poor listening, expectations regarding behavior, and scattered attention. Indeed, it seems that the more we get to know someone—our spouses, children, parents, roommates, and others—the more likely we are to take them for granted, assume we know what they are thinking or how they are going to behave, react with a short fuse, as well as a variety of other knee-jerk responses. It's as if we expect the people we love and/or live with to behave in certain ways. We then validate those expectations by noticing the behaviors we are expecting to see and either ignoring or failing to see the rest.

As an example, for quite some time I found myself expecting my daughter to object to my suggestions regarding new activities that she might like to explore. I expected her to be somewhat resistant to my preferences, and it seemed that I was almost always right. I would suggest something—and she would say, "I don't want to." Due to previous experiences with her, and because of my certainty about the way she was going to respond, I discovered that I was actually looking for verification of my correct assumptions. I blew her responses way out of proportion and read into her motives, rather than seeing each situation with fresh eyes and an open heart.

I decided to try to create a new relationship with

her surrounding this recurring pattern. I knew that the only way to do so was to explore *my* contribution to the problem instead of continuing to focus on her reactions. I looked at the ways that I was too aggressive with my suggestions. I looked at the ways that I was too aggressive with my suggestions and examined the ways I presented her with new opportunities. I discovered that the problem was, to a very large degree, me! Rather than motivating her, my genuine enthusiasm was overwhelming her. Her response to her feelings of being overwhelmed was usually to decide not to do something new. This invariably disappointed me, which encouraged me to get even more enthusiastic. You can probably imagine how much good that did. As I began to change, so too did our relationship.

The change in our relationship has been significant. I now understand that my expectations of my daughter, both for the way I felt she should respond to my suggestions and for my predictions regarding the way she was *going* to respond, represented virtually all of the problem. It turns out that she loves to try new things but prefers to do so in her own time—not mine. What she doesn't love is an overly enthusiastic father pushing her too quickly and demanding an enthusiastic response. Now that I can see what I had been doing, I don't blame her one bit! Because I have backed off from my expectations, she is now able to see that when I get too excited it's one of the ways that I show my love. Both of us are growing and becoming more accepting of the other.

13.

Remember to Show Your Appreciation

Without question, one of the primary sources of resentment in most marriages—indeed, in most family relationships—is the feeling of being taken for granted, of not feeling appreciated. Sadly, many of us are so used to being around our family members that we forget to show each other how much we appreciate one another. We take each other for granted. Kids do it to their parents and vice versa; spouses are notorious for failing to demonstrate appreciation.

I have friends and acquaintances who have very loving parents who take time and energy to take care of their young grandchildren for evenings, even entire weekends, yet I've never seen my friends show the slightest appreciation for this monumental effort. The attitude seems to be "They should want to do it. After all, they are my children's grandparents." It's easy to forget that everyone wants and needs to feel appreciated—even grandparents. It's so important and so incredibly easy to do. Not feeling appreciated is one of the major sources of burnout. I've seen a lack of appreciation destroy marriages, parent-child relationships, and sibling-sibling (as well as every other type of family) relationships.

My suggestion here is very simple. Whenever the opportunity presents itself, and whenever there is the slightest indication that it's appropriate to show your appreciation, bend over backward to do so. Say "Thank you" often, and from your heart. Write thank-you cards and do nice things for others who do nice things for you.

Last weekend, I was privileged to deliver part of a eulogy. My wife's great-uncle Miles, whom we all loved dearly, had passed away a few days before. He meant so much to the entire family that he will be dearly missed.

Just today, Kris and I received a beautiful note from Miles's son and daughter-in-law. In part, the letter read, "Richard, Miles loved you from the first time he met you. He described you as a fine person and as the only young person who had taken the time to write a thank-you note after you first visited his lake cabin." That's the power of appreciation. Miles had remembered something as simple as a thank-you for the rest of his life. It stood out because gratitude is somewhat rare in our culture.

When someone feels appreciated, he or she is so much happier and easier to be around. If you have kids, let them know that you appreciate them. Kris and I sometimes thank our children for being a part of our family. We really mean it too! Be sure to thank everyone else in your family as well—your parents, siblings, relatives, everyone. Let them all know how much you value them. You'll be amazed at the results. Everyone loves to feel appreciated—absolutely everyone.

In my experience, there is a direct relationship between families who demonstrate appreciation and families who stick together, physically and emotionally. Teenagers who feel valued and appreciated are easier to be around and learn to appreciate themselves. Wives who feel appreciated love and admire their husbands, and husbands who feel appreciated love and admire their wives. The same is true with siblings, both when sharing a home as well as when they are grown-up and on their own.

I have two wonderful sisters, one older and one younger. Both are great at sharing their love and appreciation for me, and I try to do the same for them. Without question, this is one of the reasons why we remain connected and make time for each other.

14.

Don't Go to Bed Mad

I learned this bit of wisdom from my parents, and I've appreciated it my entire life. While I was growing up, this family philosophy cut short, or nipped in the bud, many arguments, angry evenings, and negative feelings that would have undoubtedly carried forward to the next day, or perhaps even longer. The idea is that, despite the fact that all families have their share of problems and issues to contend with, nothing is so bad that it's worth going to bed mad over. What this strategy ensures is that, regardless of what's happening, who's to blame, or how mad you or someone else in your family happens to be, there is a set cap or limit to your anger, at which time everyone in the family agrees it's time to let go, forgive, apologize, and start over. No exceptions. this limit is bedtime.

When you have an absolute policy that no one goes to bed mad, it helps you remember that love and forgiveness are never far away. It encourages you to bend a little, to be the first to reach out and open the dialogue, offer a genuine hug, and keep your heart open. When you make the decision to never go to bed mad, it helps you see the innocence in your own behavior and in that of your family members. It keeps the channels of communication open. It reminds you that you are a family and that, despite your problems and disagreements, you love, need, and treasure each other. The decision that it's never a good idea to go to bed mad is a built-in reset button that protects your family from stress, hostility, and resentment.

Perhaps it's easier to see the importance of such a policy in its absence. Without a family policy such as this, arguments and anger are open-ended. No one will have created a boundary, a set of rules that protect your family from extended and unnecessary anger. Without a rule to suggest otherwise, family members can hold on to their anger and justify doing so.

Kris and I have tried very hard to implement this strategy in our family. While it's not perfect, and while occasionally one or more of us seems a little frustrated at bedtime, on balance it's been enormously helpful. It ensures that ninety-nine times out of one hundred, we'll wake up the next morning with love in our hearts and with an attitude of "This is a new day." I hope that you'll give this strategy a fair try. It's certainly not always easy, and you probably won't bat 100 percent, but it's well worth the effort. Remember, life is short. Nothing is so important that it's worth ruining your day, nor is anything so significant that it's worth going to bed mad. Have a nice sleep.

15.

When Someone Asks You How You Are, Don't Emphasize How Busy You Are

Putting too much emphasis on our busyness has become a way of life, almost a knee-jerk reaction. In fact, I'd guess that one of the most common responses to the greeting "How are you doing?" has become "I'm so busy." As I write about this strategy, I have to admit that, at times, I'm as guilty of this tendency as anyone else. However, I've noticed that as I've become more conscious of it, I'm putting less and less emphasis on my own busyness—and I'm feeling a whole lot better as a result.

It's almost as though we become more comfortable after confirming to others that, we too, are very busy. I was in the grocery story last night on my way home from work when I witnessed two sets of friends greeting one another. The first person said, "Hi, Chuck. How's it going?" Chuck sighed loudly and said, "Really busy, how about you?" His friend responded, "Yeah, me too. I've been working really hard."

Then, almost as if the customers in the store knew I was writing a book, two women added to my material! Not more than a few seconds later, out of the corner of my eye, I heard one woman say to the other, "Grace, nice to see you. How's everything?" Grace's response was to noticeably shrug her shoulders and say, "Pretty good, but really busy," followed by a polite and seemingly sincere "How about you?" The answer: "You know, busy as ever."

It's very tempting to enter into a conversation with these words because the truth is that most of us *are* really busy. Also, many people feel they have to be busy or they have no value in our society. Some people are even competitive about how busy they are. The problem, however, is that this response and overemphasis on how busy we are sets the tone for the rest of the conversation. It puts the emphasis on busyness by reminding both parties how stressful and complicated life has become. So, despite the fact that you have a moment to escape your stressful existence by saying hello to a friend or acquaintance, you are choosing to spend even your spare moments emphasizing and reminding yourself how busy you are.

Despite the fact that this response may have elements of honesty, it works against you—and your friend—by reinforcing your feelings of busyness. True, you're busy, but that's not all you are! You're also an interesting person with many other qualities besides busyness. The fact that most of us emphasize how busy we are to others isn't entirely necessary but is simply a habit many of us have fallen into. We can change this habit by simply recognizing that it exists—and exploring other options.

I think you'll be amazed at how much more relaxed you'll become if you do nothing more than change your initial comments to people you see or talk to on the phone. As an experiment, try to eliminate any discussion about how busy you are for an entire week! It may be difficult, but it will be worth it. You'll notice that, despite being as busy as ever, you'll begin to *feel* slightly less busy. You'll also notice that, as you deemphasize how busy you are, the people you speak to will sense permission from you to place a little less emphasis on their own busyness, helping them to feel a little less stressed and perhaps encouraging your entire conversation to be more nourishing and jointly relaxing. So, the next time someone asks you how you are doing, say anything *except* "I'm really busy." You'll be glad you did.

16.

Don't Be a Martyr

Needless to say, we all make many sacrifices and trade-offs in our relationships and family lives. Most of these sacrifices are well worth it. But, as with most things (including good things), too much is still too much.

Obviously, the tolerance levels to stress, responsibility, lack of sleep, sacrifice, hardship, and everything else are going to vary from person to person. In other words, something that's supereasy for you might be quite difficult for me—and vice versa. However, if we can pay attention to, and be honest about, our feelings, each of us knows when the level of stress has risen too high. When it does, we usually feel incredibly frustrated, agitated, and perhaps most of all, resentful. We may feel a little self-righteous and convince ourselves that we're working harder than other people and that we have it tougher than everyone else.

Many of us (myself included) have fallen prey to the seduction of becoming a martyr. It's easy to have this happen because there is often a fine line between working hard out of actual necessity and overdoing it out of perceived necessity.

The sad truth is, however, that no one actually benefits from or appreciates a martyr. To himself, a martyr is his own worst enemy—constantly filling his head with lists of things to do and always reminding himself how difficult his life is. This mental ambush saps the joy from his life. And to the people around him, a martyr is an overly serious complainer who is too self-absorbed to see the beauty of life. Rather than feeling sorry for him, or seeing him as a victim, as the martyr would love to see happen, outsiders usually see a martyr's problems as being completely self-created.

If you think you may have martyr tendencies, I urge you to give them up! Rather than spending 100 percent of your energy doing things for other people, leave something for someone else to do. Take up a hobby. Spend a few minutes a day doing something just for you—something you really enjoy. You'll be amazed by two things. First, you'll actually start to enjoy your life and experience more energy as you feel less stressed. Nothing takes more energy than feeling resentful and victimized. Second, as you let go of resentment and the feeling that everything you do you do out of obligation, the others around you will begin to appreciate you more than before. Rather than feeling as if you resent them, they will feel as if you enjoy and appreciate them instead—which you will. In short, everyone wins and benefits when you give up your victim attitude and your tendency to be a martyr.

17.

Create a "Selfish" Ritual

It has always amused me when people have responded to my suggestion that they take care of their own needs with the question "Wouldn't that be selfish?" I'd like to take this opportunity to put that concern to rest! This strategy stems from the understanding that when you have what you need, in an emotional sense, you have plenty left over for other people and their needs.

If your goal is to become more relaxed and happy at home, one of the most helpful things you can do is to create an activity that is yours exclusively, something you do—just for you. For example, my private ritual is to get up really early in the morning before anyone else in my family. I use this time to stretch, have a quiet cup of coffee, and read a chapter or two in my favorite book. Sometimes I meditate or reflect on my life. I cherish this special ritual in my day.

Obviously, everyone is different. Some people like to squeeze a little exercise into their routine—creating a healthy ritual. Others like to browse bookstores or have a quiet cup of coffee before work. Still others like to take a warm bath or shower at a predetermined time. The point is, it's your time—a special part of the day that is reserved for you.

A ritual that I used to practice, that I've shared with many others, is that I would stop a few blocks from my home on my way home from work. I'd pull off the road in an area where there were lots of trees and plants. And for just few minutes, I'd simply look at the beauty around me. Nothing fancy, not too much time. But just enough to give me a breather between my work life and coming home to energetic kids who wanted and deserved my attention. During those few minutes, I'd breathe deeply and remind myself how lucky I was to be going home to a loving family. I'd look in awe at the beautiful trees and plants. Then, after a few minutes, I'd start the car and drive home.

The difference in how I felt when I took this time was enormous. Rather than rushing in the door tired and grumpy, I'd feel relaxed and loving. I could tell the difference in my reception from my family as well. Apparently, they could sense my peace.

Whether you get up a little earlier, take a regular bath, or stop and smell the roses on your way home from work, do something. Create a ritual that is just for you. You'll be amazed at how much value you get out of so few minutes.

18.

Stop Exchanging Horror Stories

This strategy is particularly suited for people who live together. It's a common phenomenon for two people, whether they work away from the home or stay at home during the day, to come together in the evening and spend a great deal of time and energy exchanging "horror stories." More specifically, what I mean is that the bulk of the conversation is geared toward all the rotten and horrible things that went on during the day. Discussions include how difficult and tiring the day was, how many demands were placed on you, the irritations you had to face, the inconveniences, the bad experiences, the difficult moments, the demanding children, the insensitive bosses, and so forth. It seems many of us want to be sure that our spouses or living partners understand how difficult our lives really are.

There are several reasons why I believe this habit is a big mistake. First off, most of us have precious little time to spend each day with our loved ones. It seems to me that, if we have a difficult day, it doesn't make any sense to re-create it in the evening. The act of thinking about and discussing the negative events of the day is tantamount to re-experiencing them. This creates an enormous amount of stress and is emotionally draining.

Second, focusing too much on the negative parts of your day is self-validating. In other words, it serves to remind you of the pressures and difficulties of daily living, thereby convincing you that it's appropriate to be serious, heavyhearted, and uptight.

The simple act of eliminating, or at least reducing, the amount of energy you spend telling your horror stories has an almost instant and in some ways magical quality of making you feel better about your life. It's not that you don't have extremely difficult and serious things to deal with—we all do—it's just that commiserating with others about these difficult part of life costs far more than it is worth. As you let go of this tendency, you'll be reminded of the better parts of life. It will be easier to remember and think about the loving and kind aspects of life, those things that went right and went well, the parts of your life that you are proud of and that nourish you. You'll also notice that when more of your attention is on the positive aspects of your day, your spouse or living partner will quickly follow suit. Most people, when they break this all-too-common habit, find that focusing on the positive is far more interesting and a great deal more fun. New doors will open in your relationship, and new interests will develop.

Please understand that I'm not suggesting that it's never appropriate or useful to share what's going on—including the worst things—with your loved ones. At times, you may want to, or even need to. There are many exceptions to this strategy. What I'm suggesting you get away from is the abuse of this tendency. Rather than making it a regular part of your evening, something you do without question on a regular basis, see if you can reduce it to an occasional thing that you discuss. Obviously, you want to be honest about your true feelings, but I've found that it can be richly rewarding to leave some of the negative behind. Before jumping in, you might ask yourself, "What is this going to accomplish?" Or you might ask, "Is sharing this information going to brighten either of our days, or is it going to bring us down? Is it going to bring us closer, make us more intimate, or is it going to be one more reminder of how difficult life can be?"

I think we all know that life can be extremely difficult and tiring. I also believe that most of us take it as a given that we must deal with hassles each and every day. The questions are, Does sharing all the gloomy details do any good? Does it have true value? And despite the fact that I'm as guilty as anyone else of abusing this tendency at times, I've found that, a vast majority of the time, sharing negativity is counterproductive at best and an interference to a quality, relaxing evening.

I encourage you to give this suggestion a try. The next time you feel like sharing information on how horrible or testing your day has been, see if you can keep it to yourself instead. My guess is that you'll discover it to be a truly healing thing to do.

19.

Ask Yourself the Question "What Messages Am I Really Sending to My Children?"

One of my favorite parenting books is Dr. Wayne Dyer's *What Do You Really Want for Your Children?* In it, he encourages parents to ask themselves what they really want to teach their kids and to examine the hidden messages we are sending them. He suggests that some of the most important and valued human qualities—self-reliance, risk taking, patience, independence—can be hampered by the invisible ways we communicate with our kids.

Sometimes, for example, we demand that our children relax, or quiet down, but do so by raising our own voices in frustration. Or, we want our kids to grow up being independent, yet we clean their rooms out of personal frustration, or fail to allow our children to take appropriate risks. Perhaps we *say* we want our children to be calm, yet we are hyper, even frantic, ourselves. Perhaps we want our children to grow up being cooperative, yet we have a tendency to argue too often. There are many examples where we want to encourage a certain type of behavior yet we are sending a message that suggests otherwise.

So many of the messages we send our kids stem from what's going on inside of us. Are we frustrated and reactive—or are we calm and responsive? Are we patient and supportive or demanding and aggressive? Are you a great listener? Do you listen to your spouse, your friends, and your kids, or do you have a tendency to interrupt others or finish their sentences? If so, is it any wonder our children have difficulty paying attention to and/or listening to our instructions?

One of the positive hidden messages Kris and I have given to our children is that we have made the conscious decision to always keep our own relationship alive and fresh. We make plenty of time for each other and go out on regular dates. In addition to enjoying our relationship, we want our children to grow up *knowing* that their parents truly love and value each other—not just because we tell them so but because we demonstrate with our actions and behavior what a good relationship looks like. One of the things I think we need work on is our tendency to rush, yet ironically, we get annoyed when our kids are impatient. Again, the behavior in the home is affected by the hidden messages we send our kids.

Take a look at your own hidden messages and

signals. In all likelihood, there are many things you are doing well and other areas that may need improvement. Don't worry about it—welcome to the human race! The most important thing is to be aware of the power of your hidden messages. Once you are, you can catch yourself when you are sending a message that is inconsistent with what you might actually desire. With a little practice in this area, I think you'll agree that asking yourself "What messages am I really sending to my kids?" is an important question indeed.

20.

Don't Wait for Bad News to Appreciate Your Life

Eventually, many of us will receive a much-dreaded terminal diagnosis. And besides the shock that we will undoubtedly experience, one other thing is certain to occur: Our ordinary life will be experienced with heightened appreciation. The things we sometimes take for granted—laughter, beauty, friendships, nature, family and loved ones, our home—will all seem more important and special than ever before. Each day will be experienced as a gift and as a cherished miracle. What's more, all the "small stuff" that tends to bother us so much won't seem at all important or worthy of so much attention. The little aggravations that we tend to focus on will fade in significance. Our attention will be on the tremendous gift of life.

Because we know, with relative certainty, that this will be our reaction to bad news, as it has been for so many before us, what possible value could there be in *waiting* to appreciate your life? Instead of postponing your experience of gratitude until you are forced to do so by some form of bad news, why not instead begin to treasure your life right now? Life itself is a miracle, and we are truly blessed to be here.

A great deal of potential enlightenment can be found by reminding yourself how short and fragile life really is and how quickly things can change—one minute you have a spouse or a child, the next you don't. One minute you think you're going to live forever—the next you discover you will not. One day you enjoy your daily walk—the next you have an accident that makes walking impossible. One day you have a home—the next it's lost in a fire. You get the picture. Obviously there are two distinct ways to look at the uncertainty and fragility of life. One way is to feel defeated and frightened over the inevitability of change, including painful changes. The other, more positive, take on the same set of facts is to use this uncertainly as a constant reminder to be grateful.

Because we are so familiar with, and spend so much time at, our homes, it's easy to take for granted our families, possessions, environment, privacy, safety, comfort, and all the other things our homes provide us with. Because of this tendency, it's critical to constantly remind ourselves of how fortunate we are to have a home, however humble it may be. We need to take actual time (perhaps a few minutes) every day to think about and express, if possible, gratitude for the important role our homes play in our lives. Instead of waiting for bad news to make you treasure the gift of your life, if you begin to make it an integral part of your life right now, you'll experience more joy around the home than you ever felt possible. Give it a try. I'll bet you have a lot more to be grateful for than you realized.

21.

Encourage Boredom in Your Children

To the typical parent, little is more aggravating than hearing these words from their children: "I'm bored" or "There's nothing to do." This is especially true for parents who try really hard to provide their children with a variety of experiences and activities to choose from. Yet, ironically, it's the parents who try the hardest who usually suffer the most from these words.

Children who have too many opportunities, choices, scheduled activities, and things to do are often the ones who are the most susceptible to boredom. The reason is that these children are used to being entertained and stimulated virtually every moment of every day. They often rush from activity to activity with little time in between and have schedules that look almost as full as those of their parents! Very simply, if something isn't going on, they feel bored and restless, almost desperate to find something to do. Many kids feel they can't live without a telephone in their hand, a television set or radio playing at virtually every moment, or a computer or video game to entertain them.

The solution *isn't* to feed them ideas of things that they can do to alleviate their boredom. As you know, they will usually reject your ideas anyway. A bigger issue, however, is that in the long run you're doing a disservice to your kids. By offering too many suggestions about ways to keep busy, you are actually feeding the problem by suggesting that the kids really *do* need something to do every minute of every day.

A great solution (and one that will shock your

bored kids) is to respond to the "I'm bored" line with a confident "Great, be bored." You can even go on and say "It's good for you to be bored once in a while." I can almost guarantee you that, once you try this a few times and really mean it, your kids will give up on the idea that it's *your* responsibility to entertain them on an ongoing basis. A hidden benefit to this strategy is that it will encourage greater creativity in your kids by forcing them to discover things to do on their own.

I'm not suggesting you do this all the time or that you don't take a loving, active role in the activities that your kids participate in. What I'm referring to here is a response to overstimulation—when you know in your heart that your kids have plenty of things to do and that their boredom is coming from them, not from a lack of possibilities. I think you'll love the sense of authority you'll feel by putting the problem of boredom back where it belongs—with your kids. And, as important, you'll be doing your kids a tremendous favor by teaching them that there's nothing wrong with not having something to do every minute of every day. It's okay to be bored once in a while.

22.

Don't Answer the Phone

How often have you been completely overwhelmed by all that you're doing at home when, at the worst possible moment, the phone rings? Or, you're trying desperately to get out the door by yourself or with your kids when—*ring, ring, ring*—the phone calls out for your attention. Or, on the other end of the spectrum, you're absorbed in a special moment—by yourself or with someone you love—when, again, the phone rings.

The question is, did you answer it? If you're like most people, you probably did. But why? Our response to a ringing phone is one of the few things in life over which we have absolute control and decision-making authority. In this day and age of answering machines and voice mail, it's not as critical to answer the phone as it once was. In most cases, we can simply call someone back at a more convenient time.

In our home, one of the most stressful moments is when the phone rings just as we are going out the door in the morning and one of the kids runs over and answers it! Now, rather than getting in the car, I'm back on the phone addressing someone else's concern. The time and accompanying stress is rarely worth it. I've learned a little secret. I have one of those phones that has a "ringer off" feature. Sometimes, when I remember, I turn the ringer off about thirty minutes before we actually have to leave. This way, the kids won't be tempted to answer the phone.

Many years ago a good friend of mine and I were talking about the issue of answering the phone during a family dinner. We agreed that unless you were expecting a very important call, answering the phone during family time sends a hurtful message to your entire family and is, in fact, disrespectful. The message is: An unknown person is calling and it's more important to me that I answer his or her call than it is to sit with you right now. Pretty scary, isn't it?

Some of my most magical moments with my kids have been when we've been spending time together reading or playing and the phone rings. But rather than interrupting our time together, we look at each other and agree—nothing is more important than our time together right now! This is one of the ways I show my kids how important they are to me. They know I practically live on the phone and my decision to not answer it doesn't come easily.

Obviously there will be many times when you'll

want to answer the phone. I urge you, however, to choose carefully. Ask yourself the question "Is answering the phone at this moment going to make my life easier, or is it going to add stress to my day? Simple as it seems, choosing *not* to answer the phone, on selected occasions, can be a very empowering decision and can greatly reduce the stress in your home life.

23.

Make Peace with Bickering

There's nothing quite like a bickering match between siblings to ruin an otherwise peaceful day around the house. Anyone who has experienced sibling rivalry knows exactly what I mean.

It was shortly after our youngest daughter's second birthday when one of my friends suggested "You'd better get used to it" in response to my concern about squabbling that seemed to be brewing. It turns out she was absolutely right. The truth is, if you have more than one child, bickering is a fact of life. The question isn't whether or not bickering will occur but instead: What is the best and wisest strategy to deal with it?

I'm the first to admit that there are times when bickering gets on my nerves in a big way. However, I have found that the best strategy available to parents, grandparents, baby-sitters, caretakers—anyone dealing with kids and bickering—is to make peace with it, once and for all. I realize this is easier said than done, but what options do you really have?

There are two excellent reasons for making peace with bickering. The first is that when you struggle against something—anything—it makes whatever you are struggling against seem even worse than it really is. For example, if your two sons are arguing and you get overly involved, intervene too quickly, or become too reactive, you have to deal with not only fighting kids but your own reactions as well—high blood pressure, negative thoughts, and agitated feelings. When you struggle against bickering it's as if you enter the ring with your kids. This makes it easy to blow the bickering out of proportion, which is another way of saying you'll end up sweating the small stuff.

The second reason to make peace with bickering is that when you struggle against it, you actually encourage more of the same. In a way, you're sending the wrong message, even acting as a poor role model. After all, how can you be demanding "peace" from your children when you are experiencing conflict? In most cases, your kids will sense your agitation and reactivity, which encourages each child to see if he or she can convince you to take sides. Your inner struggle (or external reactions) further fuel the fire.

The good news is, the opposite is equally true. When you make peace with bickering, when you accept it as part of the package of parenting, no added fuel is thrown on the fire. In fact, there is a relationship between the degree to which you can stay detached and relaxed and the lesser amount of bickering that you will have to endure.

Obviously, there are times when you'll want or have to get involved, and, of course, you'll want to guide your children in their journey toward getting along with one another. What I'm referring to are the ongoing bickering matches that exist on a day-to-day basis. These everyday, normal conflicts are the ones that you want to make peace with. As is so often the case, our acceptance of what is, instead of our insistence that life be what we would like it to be, is the key to a more peaceful life. When you make peace with bickering, you set an example of choosing not to participate or overreact to strife and chaos. My guess is this: If you can become a tad bit more detached from, and make peace with, normal sibling bickering, your kids will quickly follow suit.

24.

Learn from Kids as They Live in the Moment

This strategy is workable whether or not you have children living at home, or even if you've never had kids of your own. You can spend time around other people's children, or simply observe them at a local park. While it's certainly not always true, for the most part children naturally live in the moment. This is especially true for younger kids.

To experience life in the "present moment" is not a mysterious endeavor, nor is it any big deal. Essentially, all it involves is putting less attention on worries, concerns, regrets, mistakes, "what's wrong," things yet to be done, things that bother you, the future, and the past. Living in the present simply means living life now, with your attention fully engaged in this present moment, not allowing your mind to carry you away to experiences removed from this moment. When you manage to do this, you not only enjoy the moment you are experiencing to the fullest extent possible, you also bring out the best in your performance and creativity because you are far less distracted by your wants, needs, and concerns.

Happy people know that regardless of what happened yesterday, last month, years ago—or what might happen later today, tomorrow, or next year—now is the only place where happiness can actually be found and experienced. Obviously, this doesn't mean you aren't affected by, or that you don't learn, from your past—or that you don't plan for tomorrow (or for retirement and so forth), only that you understand that your most effective, powerful, and positive energy is the energy of today—the energy of right now. When you're bothered or upset, it's usually over something that is over or something else that is yet to be.

Children intuitively understand that life is a series of present moments, each meant to be experienced wholly, one right after another, as if each one is important. They immerse themselves in the present and offer their full attention to the person they are with. I remember an endearing incident that occurred five or six years ago. My wife and I had hired a baby-sitter to watch our then two-year-old while we went out for the evening. My daughter and I were playing in her sandbox, having a great time together, when the sitter arrived. As I stood to leave, my daughter let out a fierce scream of disapproval. It was as if she were saying, "How dare you interrupt our fun together!" She yelled and screamed and complained that she didn't want the sitter—it *had* to be me. But, shortly after we "escaped," I realized that I had forgotten my car keys and I went inside to get them. I peeked out the back door and saw that my daughter was all smiles and laughter, playing, once again, in the sandbox. She was absorbed in her beautiful present moments. She had completely let go of the past—even though the past was only a few minutes old.

How often does an adult effectively do that? A psychologist or cynic might say she was being manipulative toward me—and there may be a grain of truth in that assumption. However, a happy person would recognize that she was simply voicing her strong objection in one moment and then moving on to the next. Once I had left the scene, she freely returned her focus to the here and now—an excellent lesson for us all.

As you take this strategy to heart, you will discover that being able to immerse yourself in the present moment is a worthwhile quality to strive for. Doing so gives you the capacity to experience ordinary events in an extraordinary fashion. You will spend far less time being bothered by life, while spending more time enjoying it. You'll spend less energy convincing yourself that right now isn't good enough and more time enjoying the special moment you are in—this one.

25.

Marvel at How Often Things Go Right

If you were to eavesdrop on a typical conversation and if you took what you heard to heart, it would be easy to believe that almost nothing ever goes right! The focus of many conversations is limited to, or at least slanted toward, the problems of the day, the ills of society, the obstacles, injustices, and the hassles of work. The emphasis is almost always on the negative or on what's wrong. There's a great deal of discussion of what's wrong with other people, coworkers, customers, investors, clients, and everyone else. The working environment is criticized, and nothing is ever quite good enough.

But have you ever, even once, stopped to marvel at just how often things go right? It's amazing.

Literally thousands of events—work related and otherwise—go right every single day, without a glitch. Everything from the vast majority of phone calls that are returned and reservations that are honored, to travel and food safety, dependency on various forms of technology, roofs that don't leak, the competency of coworkers, the interdependence of schedules, right down to the fact that most people are friendly—so much goes right. And for the most part, we take it all for granted. For whatever reasons, we choose to focus on the few exceptions. Perhaps we believe that more will go right if we focus on what's wrong. Conversely, many people are frightened that if they were to become more accepting of imperfection, then more things would end up going wrong—which isn't true.

I fly quite a bit and hear a great deal of complaining about air travel. And it's true that I've had a few horrible experiences pertaining to delays, canceled flights, lost or missing baggage, overbooking, misplaced reservations, and other hassles. However, the percentage of the time that I get where I need to go either on time or nearly on time is astonishing. Given the enormous amount of traffic volume, tight schedules, weather conditions, and dependency on technology, this is truly remarkable. For example, I can wake up in Northern California and before dinner, I'm safely in New York City, baggage in hand—most of the time. I suspect that similar percentages of good fortune are true for most business travelers.

Yet have you ever heard anyone complimenting the airlines? I'm sure that if you have, it's been the exception, rather than the norm. In the midst of a delay, we're far more inclined to become angry and frustrated, maybe even take it personally, than we are to keep in mind that everyone involved is doing the very best he or she can, and that occasional delays are inevitable. The same lack of perspective seems to be true with so many aspects of daily business. A huge percentage of people are friendly, helpful, and courteous. What you hear about, however, are the tiny percentage of people who are rude, insensitive, or incompetent. A person may have a dozen tasks to complete in a day. Eleven of them went smoothly; the other one is discussed over dinner.

I'm not going to discount the fact that there are problems to deal with; there most certainly are. Likewise, most of us must face our share of hassles, disappointments, incompetence, and rejection. It's all part of working for a living. It seems that we've become so accustomed to things going smoothly, however, that we expect near-perfection. When we don't get it, we go crazy.

I think it's wise to keep at least a little bit of perspective. When I remind myself of how often things actually go right, it really helps me deal with those things that don't. It allows me to make allowances for the fact that "stuff happens," people make errors. Mother Nature does her thing, and things do sometimes go wrong. What else is new? When I focus on how often things go right, it opens my eyes to the bigger picture and keeps me from sweating the small stuff. I think the same will be true for you as well.

26.

Learn to Delegate

For obvious reasons, learning to be a better delegator can make your life easier. When you allow others to help you, when you put your faith in them and trust them, it frees you up to do what you do best.

I've found, however, that many people—even very high-achieving, talented, and successful people—are often very poor delegators. The feeling is, "I might as well do it myself—I can do it better than anyone else." There are several major problems with this attitude. First of all, no one can do all things or be two places at once. Sooner or later, the magnitude of responsibility will catch up with you. Because you're so scattered, you'll be doing a lot of things, but the quality of your work will suffer. Learning to delegate helps to solve this problem by keeping you focused on what you're most qualified to do and that which you enjoy doing. In addition, when you don't delegate properly, you aren't allowing others the privilege of showing you what they can do. So, in a way, it's a little selfish.

Jennifer is a mortgage broker in a busy downtown office. Ironically, one of her biggest problems may have been that she was talented and highly competent at practically everything! She felt so secure about her ability to accomplish tasks, that she had become frightened at delegating almost any authority or responsibility. Whether it was making phone calls, negotiating with lenders, communicating with clients, or filling out paperwork, she was involved and on top of it all.

For a while, she managed to juggle things pretty

well. As the years went by, however, and her time became more in demand, her unwillingness to delegate responsibility began to catch up with her. She was making more mistakes and becoming increasingly frustrated, forgetful, and stressed out. The people she worked with claimed she had become more short-tempered and arrogant.

At a seminar designed to help her prioritize more effectively, it became obvious to her that her greatest professional weakness was her unwillingness to delegate and share responsibility. She learned the obvious—that no one can do everything indefinitely, and keep doing it well.

As she began to delegate responsibility—little things as well as those more important—she began to see light at the end of the tunnel. Her mind calmed down, and she began to relax. She could see more clearly where her talent could be used and where her time was best spent. She told me, "I'm back to my old self again."

Often it not only helps you but someone else when you delegate at work. When you ask for help, share responsibility, or delegate authority, you are often giving someone a chance to show you, or someone else, what they can do. In the publishing world, a senior editor might allow an associate editor to do some editing on a particular book, even though it's one of her favorite authors. This not only frees the senior editor's time, it also gives the associate editor a chance to show what she can do—so that she can enhance her career. My friends in the legal and corporate worlds say it works in the same way. Partners in law firms delegate a great deal of work to younger lawyers. Managers of corporations do the same to their less-experienced coworkers. I know that a cynic will say, "The only reason people delegate is to shove off the tough and dirty work on others." And, yes, there are plenty of people who look at it that way—but you don't have to. The point is, there are good reasons—in addition to selfish ones—to practice delegation.

I've seen flight attendants who are masters at delegation. Somehow they are able to get everyone working as a team, so that everyone's job is a bit easier. I've seen others who insist on doing everything themselves. They are the ones who seem the most stressed, and who make the passengers wait the longest. I've seen great chefs delegate certain chores—chopping, for instance—not because they don't like to do it, but because it allows them to focus on other aspects of food preparation that they excel at.

Whether you work in a restaurant, office, airport, retail outlet, or practically anywhere else, learning to delegate can and will make your life a bit easier. Obviously, there are select professions and positions that don't lend themselves well to delegation. For a good number of people, there's no way to say, "Here, you do it." If you fall into this category, perhaps you can practice at home. Can your spouse or roommate help you? Can you delegate certain chores to your kids? Might it be a good idea to hire someone to clean your home, change your oil, or something else that is time-consuming? If you think about your specific circumstances, you'll probably be able to think of at least a few ways to become a better delegator. If you do, you'll free up some time and make your life easier.

Lo mejor de Antoine de Saint-Exupéry

Saber vivir

V&R EDITORAS

No podemos prever
qué es importante en la vida.
La **alegría más grande**
se experimenta siempre
cuando menos la esperamos.

TIERRA DE HOMBRES

Vivir significa
nacer poco a poco.
¡Sería demasiado fácil
que tomemos prestadas
almas ya completas!

PILOTO DE GUERRA

Construir el futuro
significa construir el presente.
Es crear un deseo para hoy,
que se dirija rumbo al mañana.

CIUDADELA

Cuando se quiere
ser ingenioso
ocurre que se miente
un poco.

El Principito

Sin duda, cuando uno viaja,
busca tomar distancia.
Pero la distancia no se deja
encontrar. La distancia se crea.
Y la huida jamás
ha conducido a ninguna parte.

PILOTO DE GUERRA

A veces no hay inconveniente en dejar el trabajo para más tarde.

EL PRINCIPITO

Conocer no significa analizar,

ni explicar.

Es acceder a una visión.

Pero para ver,

es necesario participar.

Y este es un aprendizaje difícil.

PILOTO DE GUERRA

No encontrarás la paz
si no cambias las cosas.
Si no te conviertes
tú mismo en vehículo,
camino y movimiento.

CIUDADELA

Nunca hay
que escuchar
a las flores.
Hay que mirarlas
y aspirar
su aroma.

El Principito

No se puede inferir ***verdades***
solo mediante razonamientos,
hay que experimentarlas.

TIERRA DE HOMBRES

Es mucho más
difícil juzgarse
a sí mismo
que a los demás.

El Principito

La palabra
es fuente de malentendidos.

El Principito

Fui comprendiendo cada vez
con más claridad
que no se debe
escuchar a las personas,
sino **entenderlas**.

CIUDADELA

Reconocer una verdad
tal vez es solo
contemplarla en silencio.

CIUDADELA

He aquí mi secreto.
Es muy simple:
no se ve bien
sino con el corazón.
Lo esencial es invisible
a los ojos.

El Principito

Solo exciste una alegría verdadera:

relacionarse con la gente.

TIERRA DE HOMBRES

El niño
solo te toma
de la mano
para enseñarte.

Ciudadela

Solo lo desconocido nos asusta.
En cuanto lo enfrentamos,
deja de ser desconocido,
sobre todo si lo observamos
con seriedad y lucidez.

TIERRA DE HOMBRES

Lo que otros han logrado,
también lo conseguirás tú.

TIERRA DE HOMBRES

Algunas personas pasan toda su vida estancadas en sus asuntos, pero otras se atreven a recorrer con total certeza **un camino** en una dirección determinada.

Tierra de hombres

Solo sabemos que hay situaciones inesperadas que potencian nuestra imaginación.

TIERRA DE HOMBRES

La maravilla del hogar
donde nacimos no consiste
en que nos cobija y calienta,
ni en el orgullo de poseerlo.
Adquiere su valor porque atesora
reservas de felicidad,
porque concentra en lo más hondo
del corazón esa fuente oscura
de la que manan los sueños.

TIERRA DE HOMBRES

Al fin y al cabo, siempre vamos hacia lo que nos atrae.

PILOTO DE GUERRA

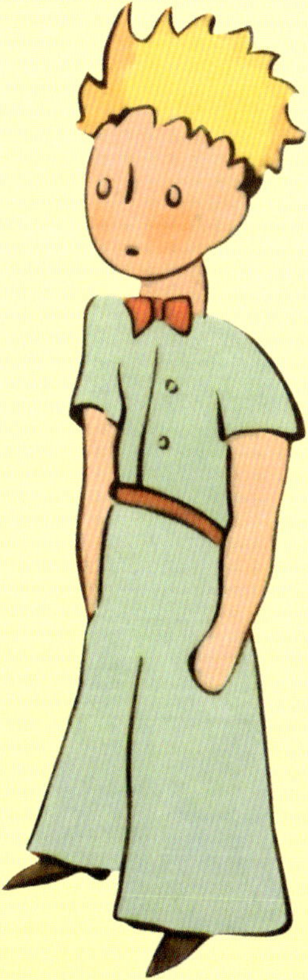

Título original: *Lebensweisheiten*
Adaptación: María Inés Linares
Armado: María Natalia Martínez

Traducción de las citas de Antoine de Saint-Exupéry, aprobada por SOGEX: María Inés Redoni

Títulos originales de las obras citadas:
Terre des hommes, 1939
Pilote de guerre, 1942
La Citadelle, 1948

Argentina: San Martín 969 10° (C1004AAS)
Buenos Aires • Tel./Fax: (54-11) 5352-9444
y rotativas • e-mail: editorial@vreditoras.com

México: Dakota 274, Colonia Nápoles
CP 03810 - Del. Benito Juárez, México D. F.
Tel./Fax: (5255) 5220-6620/6621
e-mail: editoras@vergarariba.com.mx

ISBN: 978-987-612-497-3

Impreso en Malasia • Printed in Malaysia

Marzo de 2016

Saint-Exupery, Antoine de
Saber vivir / Antoine de Saint-Exupery. - 1a ed . 1a reimp. - Ciudad Autónoma de Buenos Aires : V&R, 2016.
56 p. ; 12 x 12 cm.

Traducción de: María Inés Redoni.
ISBN 978-987-612-497-3

1. Libro de Frases. I. Redoni, María Inés, trad. II. Título.
CDD 808

¡Tu opinión es importante!
Escríbenos un e-mail a **miopinion@vreditoras.com**
con el título de este libro en el **"Asunto"**.

Conócenos mejor en: **www.vreditoras.com**
facebook.com/vreditoras

Le Petit Prince® El Principito®

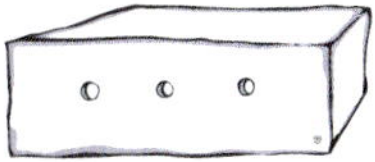

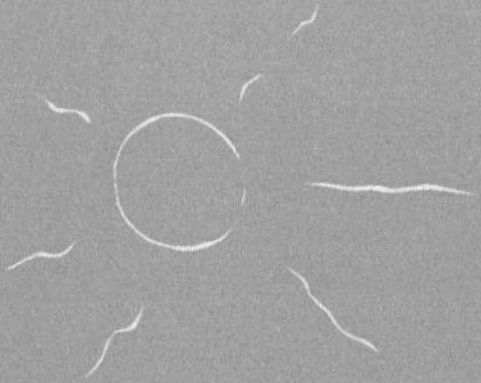